KU-400-058

Let's get moving
on safari

Emma Lynch

CHESHIRE
LIBRARIES AND MUSEUMS

1 0 JAN 2005

ASW

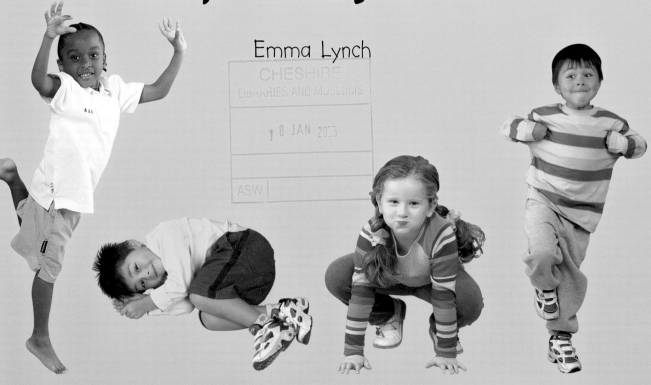

Heinemann
LIBRARY

Little Nippers

www.heinemann.co.uk/library
Visit our website to find out more information about **Heinemann Library** books.

To order:
☎ Phone 44 (0) 1865 888066
 Send a fax to 44 (0) 1865 314091
💻 Visit the Heinemann Bookshop at www.heinemann.co.uk/library to browse our catalogue and order online.

First published in Great Britain by Heinemann Library, Halley Court, Jordan Hill, Oxford OX2 8EJ, part of Harcourt Education.
Heinemann is a registered trademark of Harcourt Education Ltd.

© Harcourt Education Ltd 2004
The moral right of the proprietor has been asserted.

All rights reserved. No part of this publication may be reproduced, stored in a retrieval system, or transmitted in any form or by any means, electronic, mechanical, photocopying, recording, or otherwise, without either the prior written permission of the publishers or a licence permitting restricted copying in the United Kingdom issued by the Copyright Licensing Agency Ltd, 90 Tottenham Court Road, London W1T 4LP (www.cla.co.uk).

Editorial: Jilly Attwood and Kate Bellamy
Design: Jo Hinton-Malivoire
Models made by: Jo Brooker
Picture Research: Rosie Garai and Emma Lynch
Production: Séverine Ribierre

Originated by Dot Gradations
Printed and bound in China by South China Printing Company

ISBN 0 431 16478 9 (hardback)
08 07 06 05 04
10 9 8 7 6 5 4 3 2 1

ISBN 0 431 16483 5 (paperback)
08 07 06 05 04
10 9 8 7 6 5 4 3 2 1

British Library Cataloguing in Publication Data
Lynch, Emma
Let's get moving... on safari
591.5'09153
A full catalogue record for this book is available from the British Library.

Acknowledgements
The publishers would like to thank the following for permission to reproduce photographs: Alamy pp. **14a** (Magdy Aly), **6a** (Winifried Wisniewski); Corbis pp. **10a** (Tom Brakefield), **16a** (Michael & Patricia Fogden), **5a** (Paul A. Souders); Corbis/ Royalty Free pp. **4a**, **7a**, **11a**, **15a**, **17a**, **18a**, **19a**, **20a**, **21a**, **23**; Getty Images pp. **8a** (Digital Vision), **9a** (photodisc); Harcourt Education Ltd pp. **4b**, **5b**, **6b**, **7b**, **8b**, **9b**, **10b**, **11b**, **12b**, **13b**, **14b**, **15b**, **16b**, **17b**, **18b**, **19b**, **20b**, **21b**, **22** (Tudor Photography); NPL pp. **12a** (Tony Heald), **13a** (Francois Savigny).

Cover photograph reproduced with permission of NHPA/ Daryl Balfour.

Our thanks to Annie Davy for her assistance in the preparation of this book.

Every effort has been made to contact copyright holders of any material reproduced in this book. Any omissions will be rectified in subsequent printings if notice is given to the publishers.

The paper used to print this book comes from sustainable resources.

Contents

Going on safari

Reach up **high** and stretch your arms out **wide** like a beautiful tree.

swish!

swish!

Sway like the grass
in a gentle breeze.

Across the grassland

Stretch your body and **roar** like a lion.

mane

Rrrrroooaaarrrr!

Walk like an elephant swinging your trunk.

High and low

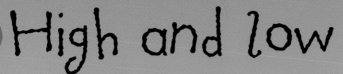

Climb high
like a monkey.

Swoop low like a vulture looking for food.

In and out of danger

Prowl like a hungry hyena looking for a snack.

Gallop like a
zebra – don't
look back!

Running

Can you run as *fast* as an ostrich?

Run and jump like a springbok.

Down to the waterhole

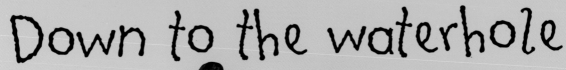

Follow my leader down to the waterhole.

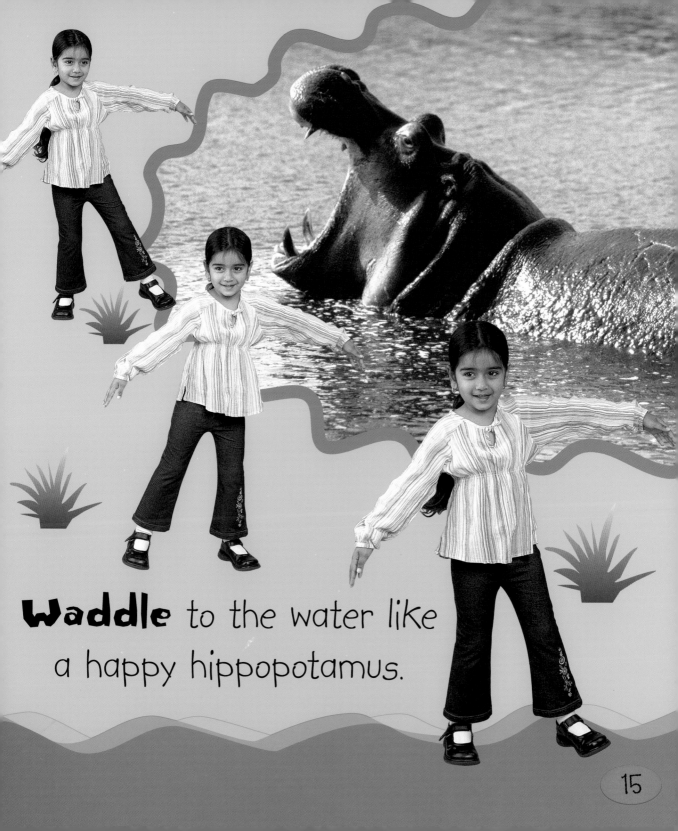

Waddle to the water like a happy hippopotamus.

15

At the water's edge

Stand on one leg and balance like a flamingo.

Snap!

Snap!

Can you smile
like a crocodile?

Hunting

Creep through the long grass
like a hunting cheetah.

Stop, start, stop, start,
swish, swash, sssshh!

Leap high into the air like a lion to catch your prey.

19

Lunchtime

Stretch up to the high leaves like a long-necked giraffe.

Bend down to
the ground and
root around
like a warthog.

Naptime

Even snakes get tired, so curl into a ball and have a rest.

Index

The end

Notes for adults

Let's get moving! explores the many different ways humans can move and encourages children to take part in physical activity. *Let's get moving!* also supports children's growing knowledge and understanding of the wider world, introducing them to different plants and animals and the way they move and grow. Used together, the books will enable comparison of different movements and of a variety of habitats and the animals that live in them.

The key curriculum Early Learning Goals relevant to this series are:
Early Learning Goals for movement
• Move with confidence, imagination and in safety
• Move with control and coordination
Early Learning Goals for sense of space
• Show awareness of space, self and of others
Early Learning Goals for exploration and investigation
• Find out about and identify some features of living things

This book introduces the reader to a range of movements used by animals on the African savannah. It will also help children extend their vocabulary as they hear new words like *swoop* and *prowl*. You may like to introduce and explain other new words yourself, like *species*, *habitat* and *conservation*.

Additional information

Most living things can move. Humans and many other animals have skeletons and muscles to support and protect their bodies and to help them move. Safari often refers to a trip to see animals in their natural habitat. Most trips take place in the African savannah, which is a grassy plain. There is typically a wet and dry season in savannah places with rain in the summer months, and almost completely dry winters.

Follow-up activities

• Can the children think of other animals from the African savannah? Try to copy their movements.
• Select one of the animals mentioned, for example elephants, to do a class project on. Find out about their lifecycles, what they eat, and how they live.
• Draw, paint or make models of the animals that live in the African savannah.